Your Amazing Itty Bitty™ Spirituality Book

15 Key Steps to Discovering the Divine Within

Summer Albayati

Published by Itty Bitty™ Publishing
A subsidiary of S & P Productions, Inc.

Copyright © 2024 **Summer Albayati**

All rights reserved. No part of this book may be reproduced or transmitted in any form or by any means, electronic or mechanical, including photocopying, recording or by any information storage and retrieval system, without written permission of the publisher, except for the inclusion of brief quotations in a review.

Printed in the United States of America

Itty Bitty Publishing
311 Main Street, Suite D
El Segundo, CA 90245
(310) 640-8885

ISBN: 978-1-7322946-6-0

Your Amazing Itty Bitty™ Spirituality Book

15 Key Steps to Discovering the Divine Within

Are you having a difficult time in your life right now? Are there unmet goals you haven't yet achieved? Are you searching for answers to questions you don't even know how to formulate?

The journey of self-discovery requires courage. Now is the time to uncover your completeness, overcome limiting obstacles, claim your power, connect with the divine within you, and attain peace of mind.

In her book, Rev. Summer Albayati helps you to recognize your true divine nature. She will guide you through the steps that will help you:

- Visualize dreams into reality
- Gain abundant living
- Lead you to your true self
- Set up a good spiritual support system
- And so much more

Unlock greater spiritual awareness and embrace your true self by grabbing a copy of this enlightening Itty Bitty™ book today!

Dedication

I thank the Divine Spirit or God, who is known by many sacred names across religions. Thank you for leading me on a journey of healing as I found my own divine power within.

I also thank my parents, Saadoun and Barbara Al-Bayati who always believed in me, even when I doubted myself and my own gifts and power.

Thank you to all the mentors along the way who shaped me into the person I have become. May I always represent you well.

Thank you to my family: my brother Nadim, my sister-in-law Marie, and my beautiful niece and nephew, Aisha and Cully. Thank you to my friends who have always been there for me. You know who you are.

Thank you to Itty Bitty™ Publishing for saying yes and being patient with me throughout this process. You are a gift to this world. Thank you so much.

Thank you to my beloved son, Devin, who is the biggest blessing in my life, and the greatest gift I could bring into this world.

You inspire me to be better than I have ever been in my life. I could not achieve as much as I do without your love and guidance. I love you so much, Habibi.

And to the ancestors, thank you for teaching me how to survive.

Stop by our Itty Bitty™ website to find interesting blog entries regarding spirituality.

www.IttyBittyPublishing.com

Or visit Summer Albayati at summeralbayati.com

Table of Contents

Introduction

Step 1.	The One Thing You Can Do to Discover Your Own Divinity Right Now!
Step 2.	Gut the Rut: Why New is Better Than Old
Step 3.	Visualizing Dreams Equals Reality
Step 4.	Stop Saying I Can't Because You Most Certainly Can!
Step 5.	Why Self-Care is the Most Important Step in This Book
Step 6.	Helping Others Leads to Your True Self
Step 7.	Don't Worry, Be Happy: The Universe Has Your Back
Step 8.	Gratitude Means Abundant Living, Not Abundant Leaving
Step 9.	Everything Begins With Belief
Step 10.	Discipline Like a Soldier
Step 11.	Travel to Experience the Holy
Step 12.	Set up Support Systems Like a Good Bra
Step 13.	Nature Lovers Unite
Step 14.	Seek Spirit on Retreat
Step 15.	Find a Spiritual Director/Companion/ Coach and Start Healing Yourself Right Now

Introduction

The journey toward wholeness is a courageous act. It is what we call a sense of spirit or unity that calls you toward your true self. Perhaps you are searching for something, or you're having a difficult time. I believe it is no accident that you have picked up this book at this moment.

I have observed many people who haven't realized everything they want to achieve in the world. What stops them? Perhaps it's self-esteem issues, or life's circumstances took them down a very different path. It doesn't matter what you are facing; you are here. Divine spirit led you here. Picking up this book is the first step toward wholeness to make all your dreams come true.

No matter what you suffer from, these pages will provide you with simple steps to overcome your obstacles and achieve peace of mind. We will take this journey together; you are not alone. Let us begin a journey to discover your own power, the divine within to become your most authentic self.

Welcome!

Step 1
The One Thing You Can Do to Discover Your Own Divinity Right Now!

Do you know who you truly are? Do you want to find more meaning in life? Sometimes you find yourself in situations that leave you with more questions than answers. That's when spirit or divine energy tells you it's time to learn more about yourself. In so doing you ready yourself for the change you need. You're wondering who you are, aren't you? Here are some ways to discover who you are today to embrace your inner strength and power.

1. Journal to help figure out what you believe.
2. Each morning, find a quiet spot and start writing about anything you want.
3. If you can't figure out what to write about, give yourself a prompt.
4. A good prompt gets you out of your head and into your heart.
5. Here is one to ask yourself: Who is God to me?

Other Things You Can Do to Find the Divine Within

Besides journaling and contemplating big questions like, *What is the source of my power?* and *How can I tap into that source every day?* you can try other exercises.

- Read books on spirituality.
- Sometimes reading generates questions and answers, which will help you understand yourself better.
- Try new spiritual practices; there are so many out there. You can try anything, but why not try something you never heard of, like Ho'oponopono? This is the ancient Hawaiian practice of forgiveness and reconciliation that brings healing to self and others. This tradition teaches that we're deeply connected to the earth and one another. Learn how interdependence with the environment helps you find the divine within.
- Try meditation, which can be as simple as closing your eyes in silence while listening to sounds around you, or enjoy a guided meditation.
- Try chanting a mantra (a repeated word or sound to aid concentration) in another language.
- Drumming, dancing, or other artistic expressions can also provide a meditative experience.

Step 2
Gut the Rut: Why New Is Better Than Old!

Have you ever felt like you're in a rut, wondering about your purpose in life? During those times divine energy (spirit) announces that you're ready for a new adventure. Think about it. If you are enjoying yourself and feeling adequately challenged, why would you try something new? That's why you need the occasional challenge to step out of your comfort zone. The following are just a few ideas to help you get out of the known to find new enjoyment in life. Who knows what amazing experiences will lead you to spirit?

1. Take a class at your local community college.
2. Start a new business.
3. Try something new you haven't done before.
4. Do something artistic like painting or dancing.
5. Make a decision and take it for a test drive to see if it's a fit for you.

What Stops You: Gut the Rut

So many people are fear-based day in and day out, afraid to take a chance or go out on a limb. While I agree that taking chances can be scary, it takes a leap of faith to try something new. Faith means you believe, unafraid of what the outcome will be. Is there something you've wanted to try for a long time but lacked the courage to jump? Why not jump today? What do you have to lose?

- Take a chance—leap into the unknown!
- Do something wild you've been afraid to do. This is the jump-out-of-an air-plane scenario.

You may be frozen, finding it difficult to act. What makes you too frozen to move? Is it fear of the unknown? What little thing can you do today to get closer to what you want to achieve?

- Incremental goals help you take steps toward the big action goal.
- Taking steps to overcome your fears is exhilarating, encouraging you to take the next step.
- When you take action and succeed, you'll find your courage increases that much more, and so does your faith.

Step 3
Visualizing Dreams Equals Reality

The divine (God, Goddess, universe, earth, energy, the ultimate, the still small voice, ancestors) are forces that guide you in life, known by many names across cultures. They want you to achieve your dreams with strength and courage. You can achieve what you want in life by exploring ideas to realize your own strength and the divinity within you

1. Write down your goals; be specific and descriptive to visualize them clearly.
2. Challenge yourself to obtain a goal and set a specific date.
3. Take one goal a day and sit in silence to visualize its successful achievement.
4. Go to a location that helps you envision the reality you desire.
5. Create a vision board with photos of things you desire. Place it where you will see it every day. Make it real by visualizing it throughout the day.

Visualize Daily to Discover Your Divinity

You're important! So spend time with yourself to discover exactly what you want in life.

- When you meditate, visualize and pray about your goal.
- This is your time to discover what the divine wants you to know.

Write down the steps needed to achieve your goal and take daily steps to make it happen.

- Remind yourself what you want to accomplish; remember that each step brings you closer to the goal.
- Act courageously to advance.
- Every day is a new opportunity to take active steps toward your goals.

Every action brings you closer to your goals and your higher self. Know that all is well with the world. That is divinity—you at your best in alignment with what the universe wants for you. This is what it means to find your inner power to become your authentic self. A great 13th century Sufi Islamic scholar and poet, Jalal al'Din Rumi, said that every bit of dust dances in ecstasy. When you feel like dancing as a bit of dust does, that is your inner divinity coming alive.

Step 4
Stop Saying *I Can't* Because You Most Certainly Can!

Many people struggle with harmful self-talk that keeps them from moving forward in life. Whether it stems from past conditioning or life experience, you have the power to prevent memories from dictating your life.

1. Give yourself permission. *I give myself permission to...*
2. Begin and end each day with positive affirmations.
3. Remember that you are love and light, so take daily steps to live and embody your true self.
4. Engage only in positive messaging and refuse to entertain negativity.

Embody an "I Can" Attitude

Remember that you have the power to change your life by choosing to engage in positive beliefs about yourself. However, you must take that power and own it for yourself.

- Post positive affirmations everywhere as reminders!
- Begin each day by loving yourself, your body, and your mind.
- Do you need to exercise more or eat better? Begin your day by taking care of yourself because you are so important for your success.

What do you need to take back the power that is your divine right in life?

- Do you need to change your routine? Do you need to focus on believing in yourself?
- Give yourself positive affirmations and believe them.
- When anxious memories flood your mind, do something nice for yourself and focus on your body. Go for a walk in nature or get a massage. Focus on taking care of yourself.

Step 5
Why Self-Care is the Most Important Step in This Book

There is only one you. Ask yourself, what would happen to your family and friends without you? Many people forget that well-being is critically important in order to have time and resources to care for others. Without self-care, you risk not having the reserves to help others.

1. Research shows that many people are dealing with burnout, which makes you feel discouraged and unhappy.
2. Treating yourself with kindness helps overcome the blues.
3. Society is interdependent and interconnected. If everyone remembered to do self-care, society would benefit from extra happiness, energy, and success.

How to Conduct a Self-Care Check

When was the last time you performed a self-care checkup?

- Make a list of all the nice things you did for yourself last week.
- Start a journal and list all the times you focus on yourself each day.
- Pledge to make time for self-care each week. Schedule a massage or mani-pedi, meet a friend for lunch, walk on the beach, meditate more, or spend more time doing things that make you smile and fill your soul.
- Each month look at your activities. Journal about your results and how they make you feel. Ask if friends and family have noticed a difference in you. Are you happier?
- Repeat this exercise each month and if you begin to feel burnout or get the blues, you know it's time for another self-care check.

Step 6
Helping Others Leads to Your True Self

You may need to unleash your true voice to find inner power. Your voice is one of the most powerful tools in your arsenal. Use it for good in the world by helping others and yourself. But first you need to find it.

1. Do you ever shy away from speaking up for yourself or others?
2. Have you ever felt the thrill of speaking up for others with one unified voice in a unified group and felt the satisfaction of seeing change for the better?
3. What would it be like to speak up for yourself or others all the time?
4. How does that make you feel? What need does it fulfill in you?
5. Feelings of achievement and changing your community by using your voice is a positive form of power. Helping those who cannot speak for themselves is also a powerful choice. Can you feel your own inner power now? Stay with that feeling and relive it over and over. Or better yet, *do* it again and again.

Your True Self is Your Powerful Voice

There are many who need your help due to injustices in the world. Sometimes the best way to find yourself is to speak up for others to help the world present its best self.

- Join a group that empowers you to speak up for others.
- Find volunteer opportunities that make you feel good about yourself. You might find your own true calling in life.
- Practice skills that help you identify important values, such as writing, public speaking, or taking classes on ethics and morality.
- The more you speak up for the rights of others, the more you will find your own inner power, leading the way to your own true self.

Step 7
Don't Worry, Be Happy: The Universe Has Your Back

Some of us live in a world of worry all the time. When life gets you down, it's difficult to believe that everything will be okay. Time and again, the universe reminds us that *this too shall pass.* It is time to believe it and embrace happiness.

1. Remember we spoke of the importance of positive affirmations? Sometimes we need to be reminded that positivity is a powerful force by itself.
2. If you focus and visualize on positive outcomes, chances are they will come true. The corollary is that negative thinking and visualization yields unwanted outcomes. What are you subconsciously attracting into your life? Focus on the positive to receive the things you want in life.

Happiness is a Choice

How many times have you heard this? The courage to be happy is a choice. It means you love yourself and require the best in life. It doesn't mean you won't have worries from time to time, but there are things you can you do to minimize them and focus on your own happiness. It's your choice. Make it work for you.

- You choose happiness every time you take a step to eliminate worry.
- If you need to pay some bills, make a list of practical steps to make it happen.
- Do you need to have fun more often? Schedule time for fun to relax, breathe, and reinvigorate yourself to bring success and happiness into your life.
- Do you need to make changes in relationships or in your career to facilitate happiness?
- Remember, no one can make you happy, and no one is responsible for your happiness. When you choose to be happy you do things that please you, and step by step happiness grows.

Step 8
Gratitude Means Abundant Living, Not Abundant Leaving

Do you know how amazing it is that you are alive? You were made for this life at this time. You were made to accomplish great things and live your most abundant life. Don't abandon your divine right or your divine gifts. Share your abundance with the world so the world will share abundantly with you.

1. Abundance is love, your divine right. Seek to embody abundance and spread more love and light, which will return to you tenfold.
2. An attitude of gratitude is the key to living a more abundant life.

Abundance Begins with Focus on Blessings

To embody love, start with gratitude each day. What are you grateful for when you first awaken? Make a point of starting each day with thanks for all the blessings in your life. New blessings will come your way when you remember that life is filled with abundant harvest.

- When you focus on being grateful, the universe shifts and sends more abundance your way.
- Start a gratitude journal to appreciate all the blessings in your life.
- Each time something positive happens, write it down. Review all your blessings every month.
- Share your abundance with others and encourage them to share their abundance with you. Life is all about giving and receiving because no one lives in a vacuum. We are social animals; we need each other! Community is where we learn to love and practice sharing light with the world.

Step 9
Everything Begins With Belief

Many people have beliefs that hold them back. It's important to understand that part of your divine right and purpose is being on this planet for a reason right now. To believe otherwise is to not embrace your true self. You are a gift! That's right; you're a gift to the universe. It's time to believe it deep in your bones. The world needs you to believe and take your rightful place on its stage.

1. Psychologists tell us belief is a powerful tool that can shape or reshape your life.
2. Living with unfounded beliefs slows your progress toward success.
3. Challenge those beliefs and rewrite them when you find they are simply not true.
4. "Always remember you are braver than you believe, stronger than you seem, and smarter than you think." – **Christopher Robin, Winnie the Pooh,** *A.A. Milne*

Seeing is Believing

You've heard the adage that seeing is believing. In acting, the audience will believe if the actor believes. We project our beliefs on to others. So, embrace your divine light and stop believing what you don't witness. You're made of stardust; allow yourself to shine! You are loved and you *are* love; project it everywhere.

- We hold all memories within ourselves. Sometimes an active memory is triggered in your DNA. Conduct a full body scan to see what your body tells you. What you keep in your body affects your inner belief. Utilize healthy movement to reframe old beliefs.
- As you age, you may not recognize yourself in the mirror. Do your beliefs limit you? Ask a friend to describe you based on their beliefs about you.
- It takes time to change limiting beliefs. You can work with a coach or spiritual director to help embody different beliefs that may be painful. If necessary, seek outside help to reframe them.
- You can rewrite the story of yourself and make yourself the hero to see how it feels.

In high school, I heard an incredible mantra: *I love myself; I am the center of the Universe.* This may be what you need to believe *right now*. Tuck it away and use it whenever you need a boost.

Step 10
Discipline Like a Soldier

What do successful people and soldiers have in common? They focus on discipline. To learn new things we need to focus on what we're learning. To learn a new language, you must practice it every day. In order to remember what was learned before, you have to study regularly so the routine becomes disciplined. Practice the art of discipline to see change in your life. This requires daily practice that leads to success in life.

1. Each day begin your ritual, whether it's exercise, meditation, or coffee.
2. Successful people add positive rituals into their lives every day to achieve more. They may read quotes that remind them of their own self-worth that guides their frame of mind that day. They may set an intention each morning and check in on how they did at the end of the day. The ritual is a daily practice that becomes a discipline to elicit positive changes.
3. What new ritual can you add to your life and what needs to become a disciplined act?

Ritual Leads to Divinity

The journey of the spirit begins with discipline. That's why you see daily rituals of prayer, chanting, meditation, and yoga being incorporated into spiritual practice. These daily practices bring you closer to divinity. No matter what you believe, daily rituals lead to knowledge about your divine self and your role in the world.

- Set a goal to explore a new ritual every week.
- Journal about your experience with different rituals. Which one helps you most and why?
- Spend time reflecting on how daily rituals help you understand the divine and embody more love and abundance.
- Document your weekly successes, no matter how small.
- Embody divinity and share your successes with others.

Step 11
Travel to Experience Holiness

With the advent of travel vloggers and movies depicting travel to find oneself, it's no surprise that travel fosters inner divinity by experiencing different cultures and practices.

1. Does your life feel mundane and ordinary? You may feel a sense of ennui or boredom with life.
2. As you travel, you will see life differently. View a sunset in Hawaii or sample spices in a souk in Morocco to enrich your soul.
3. Some find that meeting new people brings a sense of all that is good in the world and fills you with inner joy and peace.
4. As you experience other cultures and culinary tastes, your senses awaken to a new way of living and appreciating.
5. The important thing is to find good people to guide and teach you about their culture. Be open and search for the holy.

Divinity Awaits in Extraordinary Experiences

When was the last time (or the first time) you felt a divine force of absolute unconditional love all around you? When did you last smell a scent that brought you back to a time that made you happy? When did you last hear sounds reminding you that there's goodness in the world? Moments like those help you spread love and light in the world, and we all need more of those moments in our lives.

- An aesthetic experience can be a sign of the holy, and sometimes we need to go someplace that shows us new perspectives on culture, history, or architecture.
- Find a town that fills your senses with beauty—tantalizing food, breathtaking sunsets, or experiences that remind you of the greatness of humanity.
- If you cannot travel very far right now, start a travel fund and begin planning your next holy experience.
- Begin to dream by searching nearby towns and travel there as a tourist, experiencing the awe of its beauty, history, and culinary options.
- Invite a good friend to explore with you for a reminder that holiness is found in relationships with others.

Step 12
Set Up Support Systems Like a Good Bra

Many people value the importance of good support. Without it, you may be uncomfortable, may have a difficult time achieving in life, and sometimes need support to forge ahead when times are rough. When you move to a new area or away from family, support systems become even more critical. We need one another because we are interdependent social beings.

1. In some cultures, the experience of a large family or community that provides extra support is most important to a successful and happy life.
2. In forging your own path, you may find yourself alone. What do you need to ensure you don't feel alone? Who can you call on when you need a friend?

I Am Because You Are

This well-known African concept of *ubuntu,* the philosophy of collectivism over individualism, reminds us we need one another to survive. We are spiritual beings on a journey together. We depend on one another as we move together toward a more loving world.

- What do you need to better support you on this journey? Do you need more friends or perhaps more accountability partners? Do you need someone to talk to about your problems?
- Make a list of your support systems. Is anything missing that would round out your support network?
- Join a new group in your town. Take a class at the local community college. Find a good therapist or life coach. Get the support you need by being proactive.
- Set up appropriate support systems wherever you are in your life journey to foster a happier, more successful and reciprocal you.

Step 13
Nature Lovers Unite

Circadian rhythm indicates we were never meant to tolerate bright lights that keep us up all night, no matter how much fun we're having. Sometimes people need to reset their circadian rhythms with periodic natural experiences. If you've been feeling off lately, it could mean you need to get out in nature, so consider this permission to go out and frolic amongst the trees today.

1. When was the last time you went camping or kayaking, spent time hiking, or sitting on the beach?
2. If you feel the stress of city life, perhaps you need to spend more time outdoors in nature. We all need that reset from time to time, so why not reset now?

How Reset is Spiritual

Sometimes you need to reset when things feel stale. Try something different to open yourself to new ways of seeing the world by embracing opposites. If your idea of fun is sitting on the beach with a good book, try surfing instead. If a roller coaster isn't your thing, try the Ferris wheel. If public speaking is terrifying, recite a great speech to learn more about yourself. Spiritual reset helps you see delicious new things about yourself you never realized before. Explore another side of yourself to find a new you.

- Nature can facilitate the reset you need, beginning with a healthy lifestyle and a balanced diet. Reset your body by feeding it nutrients from nature.
- Sometimes a reset is as simple as taking a spiritual journey to unplug from the internet, people, and the demands of everyday life.
- Why not disconnect for a few days? Try a weekend alone without TV and invite more candlelight into your evening. What changes do you need to make to reconnect and reset your life?
- Every time you do something out of the ordinary, you open yourself to change in your life.
- It begins with one small act. All you need to do is set the intention for a spiritual reset, and then do that which calls you toward courage.

Step 14
Seek Spirit on Retreat

So you went on a retreat and realized how powerful it was for your well-being. Our ancestors knew the power of retreats. Whether you go to a mountain setting or lake resort, seek a quiet place to focus on yourself to find answers within.

1. Sometimes a retreat that speaks to you is all you need to find answers to your problems.
2. The prophets understood that retreating to unify with the divine helped their growth and communities. You too can do this for growth and self-enlightenment.
3. There are many types of retreats, from writing to yoga to adventure and wellness. You can connect with others or choose silence to connect with your own inner voice. Some retreats are in beautiful settings with exercise, healthy menus, and activities to develop your inner being.
4. The point is to focus in community or alone – to turn from daily life, to reflect on meditation, prayer, and growth, to connect with your inner divinity, and to strengthen your inner being.

Be More Like Your Ancestors

Your ancestors knew there was a time for work, for play, and a time for contemplation. They understood the importance of those things for survival. You exist because they survived and learned what they needed to do to ensure the survival of their descendants. You can be more like your ancestors by retreating to contemplate issues of growth, development of the future, and spirituality for yourself and your community.

- The ancestors knew how to celebrate the abundance of life. They knew that survival meant focusing on acts and principles that brought longer, harmonious life.
- It's time to learn from them and to be more like them. This is critical to the survival of humanity.
- What type of retreat speaks to you: writing, music, dancing, meditation, yoga, or something else?
- Find a time to schedule a retreat where you will have time for yourself, learn, grow, and evolve.

Step 15
Find a Spiritual Director/Companion/ Coach and Start Healing Yourself Right Now

Sometimes we feel lost. When that happens you may need to seek a spiritual director or coach to help you on your spiritual journey toward divine growth and light. Like an accountability partner, a spiritual coach helps you achieve your dreams. As a good friend, a spiritual director or companion helps you find answers to life's most important questions.

1. We all search at times. Answers can be difficult to find, and that's when you need help.
2. Sometimes you need a trusted companion to help you find answers through deep listening and compassion.
3. At other times you may need to find ways to unleash your potential and embrace your divine light to shine it on the world.

Healing Begins When You Answer Your Needs

It can be scary sometimes to reach out to others or admit you need help. The first step is to recognize that you're in need. The next step is to reach out. Everyone needs extra support periodically, and that's okay. Seek what you need, and you will find it. Your journey to healing begins when you say yes to your needs. You can begin healing today.

- Healing is a journey that sometimes requires more support.
- Find that support in a trusted spiritual director/companion/coach who can help you become your best self and live your best life. If not now, then when?

You've finished. Before you go…

Share/post that you finished this book.

Please star rate this book.

Reviews are solid gold to writers. Please take a few minutes to give us some itty bitty feedback.

ABOUT THE AUTHOR

Summer Albayati is an ordained Unitarian Universalist minister who found her own divine power through many of the steps in this book. As a spiritual director/companion/coach, she has helped others on their journeys to find their unique gifts and power in the world. As someone called to heal, Summer has experienced the power of prayer, meditation, music, dancing, and the extreme strength of ritual within community, leading to more love, abundance, and justice in the world.

Growing up as an American Iraqi Sufi Muslim, Summer has been a professional drummer since age 12, performing the sacred Sufi rhythms with her father, the legendary Saadoun Al-Bayati. She connected to the divine with music and dance at an early age, and her transformative healing experiences along the way led her on a powerful journey to her own divinity. This ultimately led to a life of service to others, bringing healing and justice to those she serves.

Summer cohosts a podcast with her son, Devin, called *The Bayat Beat.* The podcast is a commentary on society and culture with an emphasis on social justice. She has written chapters on spirituality, created healing dhikrs (Islamic chanting), and taught sacred drumming and dance to many seekers. As a minister, she guides followers to a holier, more loving life and hopes to companion with you on your journey toward healing and finding the divine within.

May your journey be filled with abundance, blessings, and always more love.

If you enjoyed this Itty Bitty™ book you might also like…

- **Your Amazing Itty Bitty™ Ordinary Shaman** by Christine Alisa

- **Your Amazing Itty Bitty™ Healing in Ways You Never Thought Possible** by Dr. Dolores Fazzino, DNP

- **Your Amazing Itty Bitty™ Relationships as a Spiritual Practice Book** by Deborah Gayle

Or any of the many Amazing Itty Bitty™ books available online at www.ittybittypublishing.com

www.ingramcontent.com/pod-product-compliance
Lightning Source LLC
Chambersburg PA
CBHW061303040426
42444CB00010B/2494